# *Little People,* BIG DREAMS®
# ZAHA HADID

Written by
Maria Isabel Sánchez Vegara

Illustrated by
Asun Amar

Frances Lincoln
Children's Books

Little Zaha was a Muslim girl who lived with her family in Baghdad – a city where past and present mixed in the most amazing ways.

From an early age, Zaha dreamt about the future…

Zaha had her own taste and liked doing things her way. When she was seven, she started designing clothes, and soon, she was working on bedroom furniture.

Zaha attended a prestigious Catholic school where children of all religions were welcome. Her favourite classes were Maths and Art.

One summer, Zaha and her family travelled to Rome. There, she discovered that the walls and ceilings of museums were works of art, too, just like the statues and paintings they held.

When she was old enough, Zaha went to boarding school
in Switzerland where everyone learned to ski.

But she preferred to stay in her room, drawing floating spaces that no one had seen before.

At university she studied Maths, and then moved to London to master in Architecture, where everyone found her quite unusual.

Zaha's ideas were new and she amazed her teachers with building designs that were not squares or rectangles – but curved shapes.

When she graduated, Zaha remained at the school as a teacher.
She challenged her students to be curious about forms and
materials, just like the great architect Oscar Niemeyer.

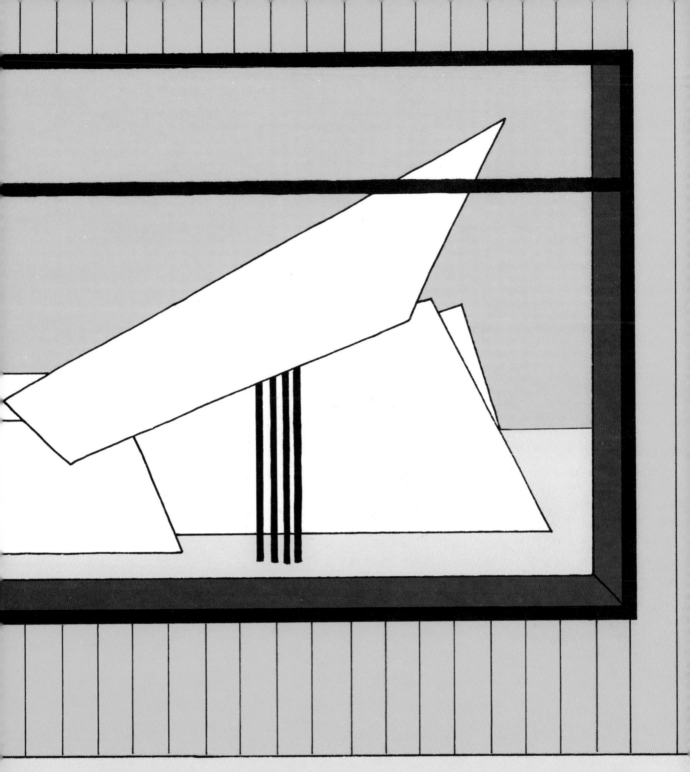

She had to wait ten long years until the first of her buildings was completed. It was a fire station made of heavy concrete that looked as light as a paper bird.

Zaha experimented with form, designing buildings that looked like giant waves, cresting on a shore made of concrete.

She convinced the best engineers to challenge machinery and build what was thought to be unbuildable.

From Beirut to Beijing, Zaha's curvy buildings changed the skylines of cities forever, creating her own map of what the future might look like.

And, she was never afraid of using computer programmes and technologies that no-one had dared to use before.

She changed the way that people thought about women —
especially an Arab woman — in an industry run by men.

PHILIP JOHNSON

RICHARD MEIER

OSCAR NIEMEYER

LUIS BARRAÇAN

KENZO TANÇE

FRANK ÇEHRY

Zaha brought a sense of femininity to the architecture world.
Her colleagues called her the 'Queen of Curve'.

RAFAEL MONEO

ZAHA HADID

REM KOOLHAAS

NORMAN FOSTER

ROBERT VENTURI

ALVARO SIZA

Zaha made it to the cover of magazines as the rockstar of architecture. She was the first woman and the first Muslim to be awarded the Pritzker Prize, architecture's highest honour.

And little Zaha – the Queen of Curve – became one of the most successful architects of her time. A true pioneer who dreamt of the future and dared to build the impossible.

# ZAHA HADID

(Born 1950 • Died 2016)

c. 1956                                    c. 2000

Zaha Hadid was born into an artistic, liberal Iraqi family. Her father, Muhammed al-Hajj Husayn Hadid, was an industrialist who co-founded the National Democratic Party, and her mother worked as a visual artist. From an early age, Zaha drew everything around her, and was intrigued when her aunt first showed her an architect's drawings when she was just 6. Zaha's international schooling meant that she was always thinking about the shape of global cities – from Beirut to Zurich – and finally London. During her postgraduate studies, she collaborated with greats such as Rem Koolhaas who spotted that she was 'a planet in her own orbit', and soon made her a partner at his practice in Amsterdam. In 1980 she opened her own practice, Zaha Hadid Architects, in London. There, she gained international recognition with work that

2013

2015

challenged how buildings were made: she wanted them to look like they were moving, and alive. In 1993, this vision was realised when the Vitra Fire Station opened. Over the next 20 years, her signature 'curve' came to life around the world, as she used the power of computers to build the impossible, creating structures such as The London Aquatics Centre, The Guangzhou Opera House or the Heydar Aliyev Centre in Baku, Azerbaijan. Zaha's personality was just as dramatic as her designs. She brought her outsider status to a profession dominated by European men, and showed her architecture peers that 'the world is not a rectangle.' Winner of multiple prizes, including the Pritzker Prize, Zaha is remembered today as a passionate feminist and trailblazer for women in architecture.

Want to find out more about **Zaha Hadid?**
Have a read of these great books and ask an adult to find
pictures of Zaha's buildings:

*The World is Not a Rectangle* by Jeanette Winter

*Zaha Hadid: Architect* by Christina Leaf

Brimming with creative inspiration, how-to projects, and useful
information to enrich your everyday life, Quarto Knows is a favourite
destination for those pursuing their interests and passions. Visit our
site and dig deeper with our books into your area of interest:
Quarto Creates, Quarto Cooks, Quarto Homes, Quarto Lives,
Quarto Drives, Quarto Explores, Quarto Gifts, or Quarto Kids.

Text copyright © 2019 Maria Isabel Sánchez Vegara. Illustrations copyright © 2019 Asun Amar.
Original concept of the series by Maria Isabel Sánchez Vegara, published by Alba Editorial, s.l.u
Little People, Big Dreams and Pequeña & Grande are registered trademarks of Alba Editorial, s.l.u. for books,
printed publications, e-books and audiobooks. Produced under licence from Alba Editorial, s.l.u.

First Published in the UK in 2019 by Frances Lincoln Children's Books, an imprint of The Quarto Group.
The Old Brewery, 6 Blundell Street, London N7 9BH, United Kingdom.
T (0)20 7700 6700  F (0)20 7700 8066  **www.QuartoKnows.com**
First Published in Spain in 2019 under the title Pequeña & Grande Zaha Hadid
by Alba Editorial, s.l.u., Baixada de Sant Miquel, 1, 08002 Barcelona, Spain.  www.albaeditorial.es
All rights reserved.

A catalogue record for this book is available from the British Library.
ISBN 978-1-78603-744-2
Set in Futura BT.

Published by Katie Cotton • Designed by Karissa Santos
Edited by Rachel Williams and Katy Flint • Production by Jenny Cundill

Manufactured in Guangdong, China CC112021

9 7 6 8

Photographic acknowledgements (pages 28-29, from left to right) 1. Family photo of a young Zaha Hadid, c. 1956 © The Zaha Hadid
Foundation 2. Zaha Hadid, c. 2000 © Alberto Heras via The Zaha Hadid Foundation.  3. Opening of the new Serpentine Sackler Gallery
designed by Zaha Hadid, 2013 © Oli Scarff via Getty Images 4. Zaha Hadid, 2015 © Kevork Djansezian/AP/REX/Shutterstock.

# Collect the Little People, BIG DREAMS® series:

| | | | | | | | |
|---|---|---|---|---|---|---|---|
| **FRIDA KAHLO**<br> | **COCO CHANEL**<br> | **MAYA ANGELOU**<br> | **AMELIA EARHART**<br> | | **AGATHA CHRISTIE**<br> | **MARIE CURIE**<br> | **ROSA PARKS**<br> | **AUDREY HEPBURN**<br> |

| | | | | | | | |
|---|---|---|---|---|---|---|---|
| **EMMELINE PANKHURST**<br> | **ELLA FITZGERALD**<br> | **ADA LOVELACE**<br> | **JANE AUSTEN**<br> | **GEORGIA O'KEEFFE**<br> | **HARRIET TUBMAN**<br> | **ANNE FRANK**<br> | **MOTHER TERESA**<br> |

| | | | | | | | |
|---|---|---|---|---|---|---|---|
| **JOSEPHINE BAKER**<br> | **L. M. MONTGOMERY**<br> | **JANE GOODALL**<br> | **SIMONE DE BEAUVOIR**<br> | **MUHAMMAD ALI**<br> | **STEPHEN HAWKING**<br> | **MARIA MONTESSORI**<br> | **VIVIENNE WESTWOOD** |

| | | | | | | | |
|---|---|---|---|---|---|---|---|
| **MAHATMA GANDHI**<br> | **DAVID BOWIE**<br> | **WILMA RUDOLPH**<br> | **DOLLY PARTON**<br> | **BRUCE LEE**<br> | **RUDOLF NUREYEV**<br> | **ZAHA HADID**<br> | **MARY SHELLEY**<br> |

| | | | | | | | |
|---|---|---|---|---|---|---|---|
| **MARTIN LUTHER KING JR.**<br> | **DAVID ATTENBOROUGH**<br> | **ASTRID LINDGREN**<br> | **EVONNE GOOLAGONG**<br> | **BOB DYLAN**<br> | **ALAN TURING**<br> | **BILLIE JEAN KING**<br> | **GRETA THUNBERG**<br> |

| | | | | | | | |
|---|---|---|---|---|---|---|---|
| **JESSE OWENS**<br> | **JEAN-MICHEL BASQUIAT**<br> | **ARETHA FRANKLIN**<br> | **CORAZON AQUINO**<br> | **PELÉ**<br> | **ERNEST SHACKLETON**<br> | **STEVE JOBS**<br> | **AYRTON SENNA** |

| | | | | | | | |
|---|---|---|---|---|---|---|---|
| **LOUISE BOURGEOIS**<br> | **ELTON JOHN**<br> | **JOHN LENNON** | **PRINCE**<br> | **CHARLES DARWIN**<br> | **CAPTAIN TOM MOORE**<br> | **HANS CHRISTIAN ANDERSEN**<br> | **STEVIE WONDER**<br> |

**MEGAN RAPINOE**

**MARY ANNING**

**MALALA YOUSAFZAI**

**ANDY WARHOL**

**RUPAUL**

**MICHELLE OBAMA**

**MINDY KALING**

**IRIS APFEL**

**ROSALIND FRANKLIN**

**RUTH BADER GINSBURG**

**MARILYN MONROE**

**KAMALA HARRIS**

**ALBERT EINSTEIN**

**CHARLES DICKENS**

**YOKO ONO**

**MICHAEL JORDAN**
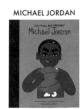

**NELSON MANDELA**

**PABLO PICASSO**

**AMANDA GORMAN**

**GLORIA STEINEM**

**FLORENCE NIGHTINGALE**

**HARRY HOUDINI**

**J.R.R. TOLKIEN**

## ACTIVITY BOOKS

**STICKER ACTIVITY BOOK**

**COLOURING BOOK**

**LITTLE ME, BIG DREAMS JOURNAL**

Discover more about the series at www.littlepeoplebigdreams.com